Teaching Little Fingers to Play
More Classics

7 Piano Solos with Optional Accompaniments arranged by
Randall Hartsell

CONTENTS

Orchestrations by Eric Baumgartner

PLAYBACK+
Speed • Pitch • Balance • Loop

To access audio, visit:
www.halleonard.com/mylibrary

Enter Code
6681-7005-0262-5083

ISBN 978-1-4950-7796-8

WILLIS MUSIC

EXCLUSIVELY DISTRIBUTED BY

HAL•LEONARD®
7777 W. BLUEMOUND RD. P.O. BOX 13819
MILWAUKEE, WISCONSIN 53213

Visit Hal Leonard Online at
www.halleonard.com

Pomp and Circumstance
Optional Teacher Accompaniment

Edward Elgar
Arr. Randall Hartsell

Pomp and Circumstance

Edward Elgar
Arr. Randall Hartsell

Play both hands TWO octaves higher when performing as a duet.

Rondeau
Optional Teacher Accompaniment

Joseph Mouret
Arr. Randall Hartsell

Rondeau

Joseph Mouret
Arr. Randall Hartsell

Play both hands one octave higher when performing as a duet.

Polovtsian Dance

(from the opera *Prince Igor*)
Optional Teacher Accompaniment

Alexander Borodin
Arr. Randall Hartsell

Polovtsian Dance

(from the opera *Prince Igor*)

Play both hands one octave higher when performing as a duet.

Alexander Borodin
Arr. Randall Hartsell

8

Optional Teacher Accompaniment

Waltz
(from the ballet *Sleeping Beauty*)
Optional Teacher Accompaniment

Peter Ilyich Tchaikovsky
Arr. Randall Hartsell

Waltz tempo

Waltz

(from the ballet *Sleeping Beauty*)

Play both hands one octave higher when performing as a duet.

Peter Ilyich Tchaikovsky
Arr. Randall Hartsell

Waltz tempo

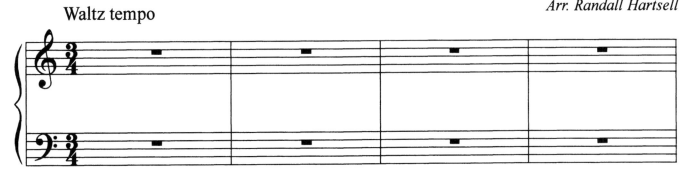

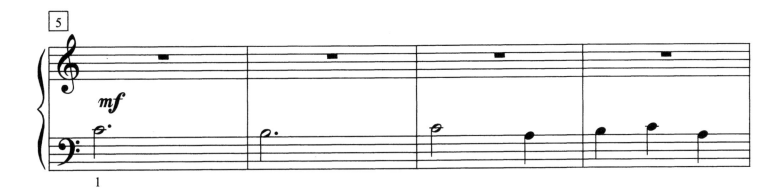

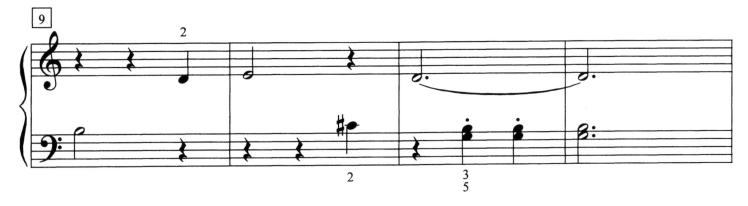

Optional Teacher Accompaniment

Marche Slave
Optional Teacher Accompaniment

Peter Ilyich Tchaikovsky
Arr. Randall Hartsell

Marche Slave

Peter Ilyich Tchaikovsky
Arr. Randall Hartsell

Play both hands one octave higher when performing as a duet.

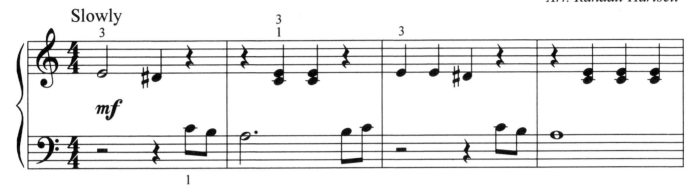

Over the Waves
Optional Teacher Accompaniment

Juventino Rosas
Arr. Randall Hartsell

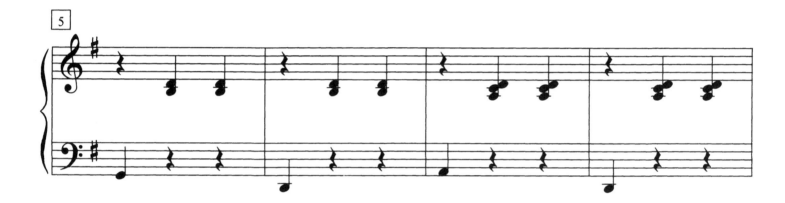

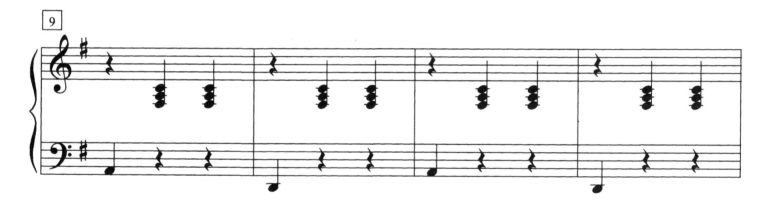

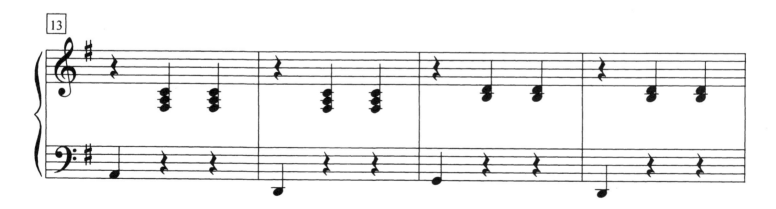

Over the Waves

Juventino Rosas
Arr. Randall Hartsell

Play both hands one octave higher when performing as a duet.

Moderately

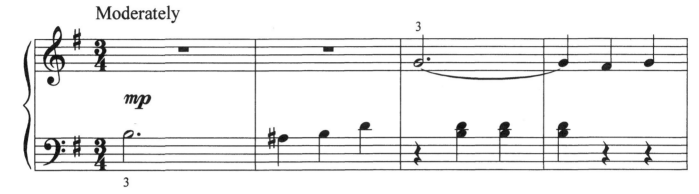

Optional Teacher Accompaniment

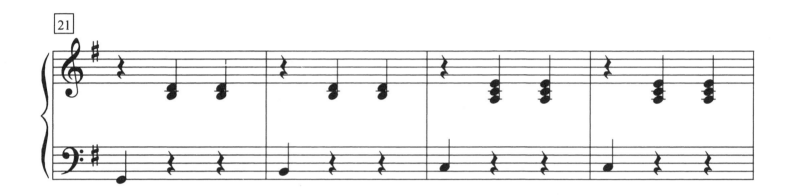

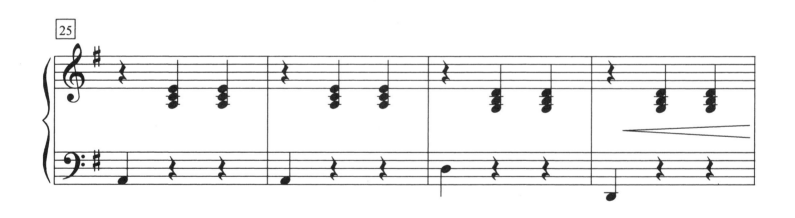

William Tell Overture
Optional Teacher Accompaniment

Gioacchino Rossini
Arr. Randall Hartsell

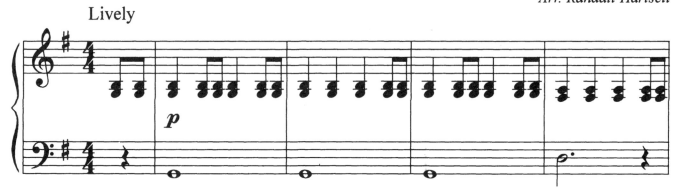

William Tell Overture

Play both hands one octave higher when performing as a duet.

Gioacchino Rossini
Arr. Randall Hartsell

Optional Teacher Accompaniment

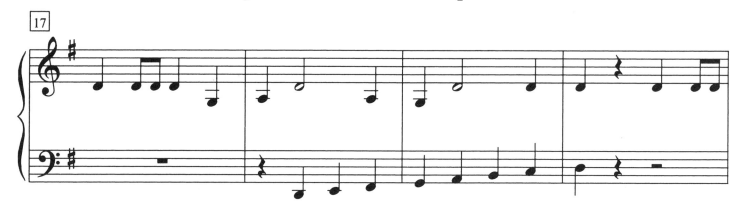

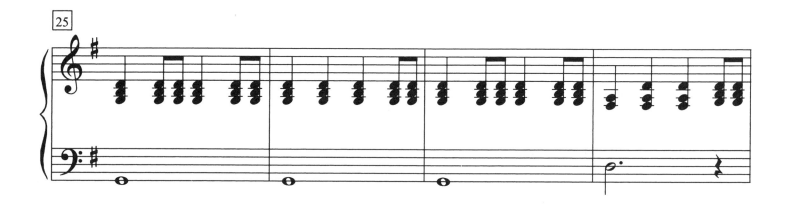

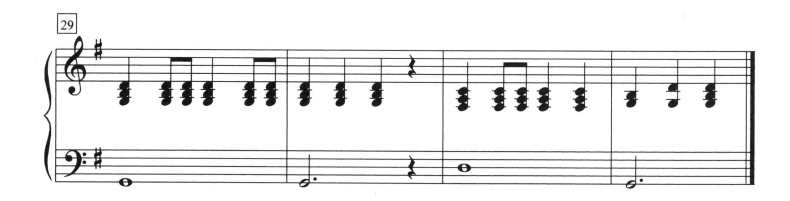

TEACHING LITTLE FINGERS TO PLAY MORE

TEACHING LITTLE FINGERS TO PLAY MORE
by Leigh Kaplan
Teaching Little Fingers to Play More is a fun-filled and colorfully illustrated follow-up book to *Teaching Little Fingers to Play*. It strengthens skills learned while carefully easing the transition into John Thompson's *Modern Course, First Grade*.
00406137 Book only $6.99
00406527 Book/Audio $9.99

SUPPLEMENTARY SERIES
All books include optional teacher accompaniments.

BROADWAY SONGS
arr. Carolyn Miller
MID TO LATER ELEMENTARY LEVEL
10 great show tunes for students to enjoy, including: Edelweiss • I Whistle a Happy Tune • I Won't Grow Up • Maybe • The Music of the Night • and more.
00416928 Book only $6.99
00416929 Book/Audio $12.99

CHILDREN'S SONGS
arr. Carolyn Miller
MID-ELEMENTARY LEVEL
10 songs: The Candy Man • Do-Re-Mi • I'm Popeye the Sailor Man • It's a Small World • Linus and Lucy • The Muppet Show Theme • Sesame Street Theme • Supercalifragilisticexpialidocious • Tomorrow.
00416810 Book only $6.99
00416811 Book/Audio $12.99

CLASSICS
arr. Randall Hartsell
MID-ELEMENTARY LEVEL
7 solos: Marche Slave • Over the Waves • Polovtsian Dance (from the opera *Prince Igor*) • Pomp and Circumstance • Rondeau • Waltz (from the ballet *Sleeping Beauty*) • William Tell Overture.
00406760 Book only $5.99
00416513 Book/Audio $10.99

DISNEY TUNES
arr. Glenda Austin
MID-ELEMENTARY LEVEL
9 songs, including: Circle of Life • Colors of the Wind • A Dream Is a Wish Your Heart Makes • A Spoonful of Sugar • Under the Sea • A Whole New World • and more.
00416750 Book only $9.99
00416751 Book/Audio $12.99

EASY DUETS
arr. Carolyn Miller
MID-ELEMENTARY LEVEL
9 equal-level duets: A Bicycle Built for Two • Blow the Man Down • Chopsticks • Do Your Ears Hang Low? • I've Been Working on the Railroad • The Man on the Flying Trapeze • Short'nin' Bread • Skip to My Lou • The Yellow Rose of Texas.
00416832 Book only $6.99
00416833 Book/Audio $10.99

JAZZ AND ROCK
Eric Baumgartner
MID-ELEMENTARY LEVEL
11 solos, including: Big Bass Boogie • Crescendo Rock • Funky Fingers • Jazz Waltz in G • Rockin' Rhythm • Squirrel Race • and more!
00406765 Book only $5.99

MOVIE MUSIC
arr. Carolyn Miller
LATER ELEMENTARY LEVEL
10 magical movie arrangements: Bella's Lullaby (Twilight) • Somewhere Out There (An American Tail) • True Love's Kiss (Enchanted) • and more.
00139190 Book/Audio $10.99

Also available:

AMERICAN TUNES
arr. Eric Baumgartner
MID-ELEMENTARY LEVEL
00406755 Book only $6.99

BLUES AND BOOGIE
Carolyn Miller
MID-ELEMENTARY LEVEL
00406764 Book only $5.99

CHRISTMAS CAROLS
arr. Carolyn Miller
MID-ELEMENTARY LEVEL
00406763 Book only $6.99

CHRISTMAS CLASSICS
arr. Eric Baumgartner
MID-ELEMENTARY LEVEL
00416827 Book only $6.99
00416826 Book/Audio $12.99

CHRISTMAS FAVORITES
arr. Eric Baumgartner
MID-ELEMENTARY LEVEL
00416723 Book only $7.99
00416724 Book/Audio $12.99

FAMILIAR TUNES
arr. Glenda Austin
MID-ELEMENTARY LEVEL
00406761 Book only $6.99

HYMNS
arr. Glenda Austin
MID-ELEMENTARY LEVEL
00406762 Book only $6.99

JEWISH FAVORITES
arr. Eric Baumgartner
MID-ELEMENTARY LEVEL
00416755 Book only $5.99

RECITAL PIECES
Carolyn Miller
MID-ELEMENTARY LEVEL
00416540 Book only $5.99

SONGS FROM MANY LANDS
arr. Carolyn C. Setliff
MID-ELEMENTARY LEVEL
00416688 Book only $5.99

WILLIS MUSIC

EXCLUSIVELY DISTRIBUTED BY

HAL•LEONARD®

Complete song lists online at
www.halleonard.com

Prices, contents, and availability subject to change without notice.

0218